New Boy

from the novel by
William Sutcliffe

adapted by
Russell Labey

AMBER LANE PRESS

All rights whatsoever in this play are strictly reserved and application for
professional or amateur performance should be made before rehearsals
begin to:
The Agency (London) Ltd
24 Pottery Lane
Holland Park
London W11 4LZ

No performance may be given unless a licence has been obtained.

First published in 2001 by
Amber Lane Press Ltd,
Church Street, Charlbury, Oxford OX7 3PR
Telephone: 01608 810024

Printed and bound by
The Guernsey Press Co Ltd, Guernsey, C.I.

ISBN 1 872868 32 0

New Boy

CHARACTERS

MARK, a sixth-former, 17
BARRY, a new boy, also 17
DAN, Mark's older brother
MRS MARGARET MUMFORD, the French teacher
LOUISE, Barry's older sister
SCHOOLBOY
SCHOOLGIRL
OLD FRIEND
GIRL AT THE DISCO
TELEPHONE ANSWERING GIRL

New Boy is designed to be performed by five actors.
The actor playing Dan also doubles as a Schoolboy.
The actress playing Louise also plays the Old Friend,
Schoolgirl, the Girl at the Disco and the Telephone
Answering Girl.

New Boy was premiered at the Pleasance Theatre,
Edinburgh on 3 August 2000. It was directed by
Russell Labey with the following cast:

MARK	Neil Henry
BARRY	Leon Parris
DAN	Josh Neale
MARGARET MUMFORD	Heather Wright
LOUISE	Lucy Bradshaw

Design by Jason Denvir
Lighting Design by Richard House

After a UK tour beginning on 23 January 2001,
New Boy was presented at the Pleasance Theatre,
London from 15 February 2001,
with the following change of cast:

LOUISE	Clare Buckfield

Scene 1

Lights up on a seventeen-year-old boy, MARK, *at a blackboard. He is alone on stage but, we gather, addressing a school assembly as if a teacher himself.*

MARK   Can anyone tell me what these are? These two curves? Anyone?

[*Pause. He looks around for an answer.*]

They are known as the outer labia. Now, you've probably all seen a pair of them somewhere or other before, and wondered what purpose they serve. Technically speaking, are they or are they not part of the vagina proper?

[*From his reaction we can tell that his audience is riveted.*]

Well, this is a matter of some contention amongst experienced lovers. It is usually agreed upon that they are, if you like, the entranceway to the vagina. To ask whether or not it is actually part thereof is rather like asking whether or not a door is outside or inside a house. The question is purely semantic. The key fact to remember is that however useful a door is for getting into a house, it must not be mistaken for the house itself. There are far more interesting things inside, concealed from the casual observer. Always remember – a courteous guest does not spend long admiring the paintwork on his hostess's porch, he heads straight for the living room, compliments her on the family portraits and warms his hands on the hearth. This little dot here represents the hearth – the fireplace – the focus of social activity. It is always further from the doorway than you expect, but it *must* be found quickly, before you (or your hostess) cools down.

[*He's clearly enjoying his reception.*]

Now – your invitation will often specify certain dress codes. Formal: condommed, or informal: *au naturel.* It is worth noting that a hostess of a social gathering will often specify formal dress simply as a matter of course. It is more important to gauge her character than to read the invitation. Often, one impresses by turning up to a black tie party in jeans and a T-shirt, so to speak. Try wherever possible to get away without wearing a condom. The experience is far better: more daring, more exciting, warmer, wetter. They only ask you to wear one as a test of your skill and enthusiasm – rather like asking a concert pianist to perform with gloves on . . .

[*A school bell rings.* MARK *switches his address directly to the audience, moving to a tightly lit spot elsewhere on the stage.*]

We were only allowed to start taking unsupervised Jewish assemblies from the start of the sixth form when it was just beginning – *just* beginning – to be cool to be clever. I had to let everyone know, as quickly as possible, just how fucking clever I was. I had spent my first five years at the school marooned in the social backwaters of the unsporty homework-doers. For the first time since we'd arrived, social status was up for grabs again. There was a tradition at the school that any new boy would be ignored by everyone except the Christians for roughly a year. It didn't work on Barry because he managed to ignore everyone else first. I have to admit that this new boy, Barry, was doing strange things to my mind – I couldn't take my eyes off him! And I couldn't help feeling that I wasn't the only one. Wherever Barry went, I could detect a little change in temperature. Even the school animal, the boy who could fit eighteen two-pence coins under his foreskin and regularly proved it – even he seemed slightly cowed in the presence of Barry. He quietened down a bit. And he certainly didn't get his dick out and start asking around for coppers. Somehow Barry put everyone on their best behaviour. I knew he'd be a useful person to have as an ally.

> [*During the following,* MARK *goes to sit down at a desk and the lights open up to reveal* BARRY *busying himself with his work.*]

Getting to know Barry wasn't easy. The mere thought of starting a conversation with him put an apple in my throat. When I actually spoke to him I had to force the words past several basketballs lodged in my respiratory system. As a result, it came out three times louder than I had intended so that Barry's first impression of me was . . . [*shouts*] Could I borrow a pencil, please!

> [*The lights close down on* MARK.]

This pissed me off. It was a very bad start. For several weeks I had nightmares in which beautiful women stripped off and offered their bodies to me while I kept my clothes on and asked them questions about pencils. Throughout my pencil impotence nightmare phase I hovered around Barry at school, hoping to find some other opening to start a conversation. Once I successfully managed . . .

> [*Lights open up again. We are now in a corridor with* BARRY.]

No, Room 63 is that way . . .

> [*Lights snap back to* MARK *in his tight audience address spot again.*]

If it hadn't been for the fortunate coincidence of Barry getting the same bus as me I don't think I would have stood a chance of ever getting close to him.

> [*Lights up on* BARRY *standing at the coach stop.* MARK *psychs himself up. Pause.*]

Cold, isn't it?

BARRY Yes.

MARK Coach is a bit late.

BARRY Yes.

MARK Mind you, it is November.

BARRY What, is the coach often late in November?

MARK No, I meant it's often cold in November.

BARRY It is.

MARK Listen – why don't you sit on the back seat? It's better.

BARRY All right.

MARK Yes! Yes! Yes! Yyyeeeaaahhhsss! Yes! Yes! Yes! Yes! Yes! Yes! My brain was having an orgasm. I couldn't believe it!

> [*Music swells.*]
>
> [*Blackout.*]

Scene 2

The changing room. Lights up on MARK. *He is sitting on a bench, with his schoolbag on his lap.*

MARK In the changing room after rugby, I was changing just opposite Barry, surprise, surprise. The thing is, I just . . . I just felt a certain manly admiration for his beauty. I think maybe I was jealous of his power to attract women. The reason why I couldn't stop thinking about him or staring at him was that I wanted to look like him so that I could have sex with lots of women. That's what it was. While everyone kept their distance from Barry, I was the one person who made the effort to get to know him – and I was amazed that he responded.

> [BARRY *enters, in his muddy rugby kit, and begins to change. He acknowledges* MARK *sitting on the bench.*]

BARRY All right?

MARK Yes . . . I mean . . . [*trying to appear casual*] . . . hello.

[*He is transfixed as* BARRY *strips and, when* BARRY *notices him staring, starts fumbling in his bag. He pulls out a bottle of shampoo.*]

Here – you can use this if you like . . . it's new . . . it's a shampoo and conditioner, sort of combined in one . . . saves you having to take two bottles into the shower . . .

BARRY [*somewhat bemused, taking the shampoo*] . . . Thanks. I'll give it a go.

[*He and* MARK *stand for a moment face to face, then he leaves to take a shower.*]

See you on the bus, then.

MARK Right. [*to the audience*] What a body! I simply couldn't take my eyes off his backside. What a fantastic arse. I didn't want to touch it or anything. I certainly didn't want to put my cock up it. I just, for some reason, couldn't stop myself looking at it. Now I'm no homophobe, don't get me wrong – but I'm also not a fucking bender. I'm not. It didn't matter much anyway because I decided not to let myself think about it. And it didn't matter to Barry because my pretty little friend was basically very slow on the uptake about most things and he didn't have a clue what was going on in my head. In fact, that's another thing I was jealous about. Nothing seemed to bother him. He didn't worry about anything. He just did things. No whingeing, like me, and analysing and agonising and moping. It was incredible! Or maybe all gentiles could do this. Whatever it was, Barry just didn't seem in touch with his own emotions.

[BARRY *emerges from the showers, wet and wearing a towel.*]

BARRY   Thought you'd have gone home by now.

MARK   Er . . . Got delayed . . . picking the root out of my verruca.

[BARRY *busies himself at his locker.*]

Actually, I'm not going home tonight. Well, I am going home . . . eventually . . . but not yet . . . parents' evening. I'm meeting them here, well, not in here, as in, in the changing rooms, but . . .

BARRY   I get the picture.

MARK   Yours coming?

BARRY   Yup.

[*He starts to get changed. After a moment's hesitation, and a glance at* MARK, *he decides on modesty, putting his boxer shorts on before removing his towel.*]

What are they like?

MARK   Both graduates, both liberal, both successful in their jobs without being too ambitious or pushy. They're both laid back about smoking, drugs and sex, and neither of them particularly bothers to tell me what to do. Can you believe it? Isn't it awful? Can you think of a more comprehensive and evil way to completely fuck up your son? Their attitude as good as puts me off tobacco, narcotics and copulation – all of which buggers up my social life. The only way I can rebel is by conforming, which is clearly no fucking good whatsoever. Worst of all, they're helpful and understanding about how difficult it must be for me.

BARRY   I meant parents' evenings. What are they like here?

MARK   An orgy of social embarrassment – I love them. It's also a good opportunity to see who has the fittest mother. Jeremy Dorlin's is quite nice, so is Robert Konisberg's, which for an ugly boy comes as a pleasant surprise – best post-forty arse in the whole of Edgware. All the Christians have ugly mothers, oh, except for yours, I'm sure, and Peter Pillow's, the vicar's son, whose mother has the subtle allure of a shaggable nun. The Asian mums are occasionally horny with the odd fit daughter in tow. All the Edgware Jewish mothers are dressed in high heels, stone-washed jeans and fur jackets with shoulder-length hair curled and dyed red. They wear so much make-up they have to pout all evening to stop it falling off in chunks. Stanmore Jewish mothers go for the drab but overdressed combo, leaving only the Hampstead and Golders Green set to dress with any style.

BARRY   And the fathers?

MARK   They fall into two groups: brown and white. Other than that they're indistinguishable. The Christian fathers are easier to tell apart, tending to divide neatly into two categories: Volvo drivers: classy – and BMW drivers: yobs made good.

BARRY   Mine drives a VW.

MARK   That's classy too. My parents hardly listen to the teachers and spend most of the interviews nervously flicking through my form list trying to figure out who they're going to bump into in the corridor next. Besides, my schoolwork's always good. My dad has only ever said one thing to me after a parents' evening.

BARRY   What was that?

MARK   'Never become a teacher.'

> [BARRY *leaves, quietly chuckling to himself.*
> *Lights close down on* MARK.]

Gradually, as we spent more time together on the coach and in the changing rooms, talking for an hour every day, we got to know each other better and better. I couldn't figure out why anyone as incredibly good-looking as him would take any interest in me. But he did. If I'd been him, I'd have been out with a different woman every night, shagging my way through the beds of north London. Why he wasn't, I just couldn't figure out, and I never got the chance to ask him because we simply never discussed sex. Or masturbation – we never discussed that either. Given that almost all my previous school relationships were based on solid, wide-ranging and frequent debates about masturbation, this was odd. How we found other subjects to discuss I'll never know. One day I came out with it. I asked . . .

> [*Lights open up again.* BARRY *is sitting on a*
> *bench with* MARK.]

What! You're a what!

BARRY   A virgin.

MARK   A what!

BARRY   A virgin.

MARK   What!

BARRY   A virgin, you arsehole, a virgin!

MARK   Fuck. I'm stunned. I can't believe it.

BARRY   Why? Aren't you?

MARK   Of course I am, you twat. Look at my face.

BARRY   What about your face?

MARK   It's ugly, that's what. It's not a shaggable face.

BARRY   You're not ugly. You're just a bit hairy, that's all.

MARK   Believe me, this is a books face. It is not a sex face.
        Now this . . . [pulls at BARRY's cheeks] . . . This is a
        sex face.

BARRY   You reckon?

MARK   You moron. What a fucking waste. What a waste
        of a face.

BARRY   I'd like to have sex at some stage . . .

MARK   At some stage?

BARRY   When I've found the right woman, I mean.

MARK   What do you mean, the right woman?

BARRY   Someone I want to spend time with – you know.

MARK   [in shock] Oh my God. What a poof! Why are you
        a virgin?

BARRY   What do you mean, why?

MARK   Why! Why, you bastard! Tell me! [getting angry]
        Listen – I am a virgin because no one wants to
        have sex with me. I am undesirable. But you . . .
        you are so . . . What have you been doing – what
        the fuck have you been doing? Are you a moron?
        [shouting] What the fuck have you been doing with
        your life?

BARRY   You're weird, Mark.

MARK   I'm sorry. It's an emotional subject for me.

BARRY   Given the chance, I suppose I wouldn't mind. You know, just doing it once and getting it over with, so I'm not in too much of a hurry when I'm looking for the right person afterwards.

MARK   You are sick. You have a diseased mind. You are pumped full of the crappiest, most outdated Hollywood sexual clichés. It's sad.

BARRY   No I'm not. I don't watch films.

MARK   What? You don't watch films?

BARRY   Not really.

MARK   What about on TV? You must watch them on TV.

BARRY   Not much. I don't really watch telly.

MARK   You don't? You don't watch telly? Do you read books?

BARRY   No.

MARK   Magazines?

BARRY   Nope.

MARK   Music? Gigs?

BARRY   Nope.

MARK   Jesus Christ! What do you do with your life?

BARRY   Dunno. This and that. You know. I keep busy.

MARK   You are extraordinary. It's unbelievable. What the hell do you do?

[BARRY *doesn't answer.*]

Listen – would you like to have sex?

BARRY   Fuck off!

MARK   Not with me, you arsehole. With a girl. With a horny girl?

BARRY   Dunno.

MARK   Don't give me that. Would you like to? Yes or no.

BARRY   Well, I suppose so, theoretically.

MARK   I'm not talking theory, Barry. I mean practically – real life – doing it – with another human being.

BARRY   Well . . . Yes. But who's going to want to sleep with me?

MARK   Jesus! Everyone. Everyone wants to sleep with you, Barry.

BARRY   Don't be ridiculous!

MARK   Listen to me, Barry. I am being deadly serious. Every single girl in the girls' school, without exception, plus every single member of staff, male and female, and most of the members of the boys' school, are all, every single one of us, desperate to jump into bed with you and screw your fucking brains out!

BARRY   Don't be silly. That's not possible . . . Really? . . . No, it's ridiculous . . . Is it true? . . . Is that what you really think? . . . No . . . you're stupid . . . Do they want to? . . . With me? . . . I mean, am I . . . ? I'm not . . . am I? . . . Do they? . . . Do they really? . . . The girls, I mean.

MARK   Yes you are. Yes they do.

BARRY   Shit. Really?

MARK   Yes, really! Do I look like I'm joking? Do you or do you not want to have sex with someone from the girls' school?

BARRY   God . . . This is . . . What are you, a pimp or something?

MARK   Yes. For the time being, I am a pimp. I will find a girl, she will come to you. The pair of you will have sex. No money will change hands.

BARRY   That's not possible.

MARK   It is possible, you idiot.

BARRY   Naaa.

MARK   Believe me. It is. All you have to do is say yes, and I'll sort it out.

BARRY   Fucking hell!

MARK   You just have to say yes or no.

BARRY   Shit.

MARK   Well?

BARRY   Fuck.

MARK   Well?

BARRY   Are you asking me to say yes or no?

MARK   Yes.

BARRY   Either yes –

MARK   Or no.

BARRY   Right.

MARK   Right.

BARRY   OK then, my answer is . . . um . . . yes . . . I think . . . but I still don't believe you . . . I mean, it won't happen . . . will it? . . . It won't . . . but yes, anyway.

MARK   [*to the audience*] The following morning, I put word out to the girls' school that Barry was a virgin, and that evening he slept with the best-looking girl in north London.

[BARRY *leaves. Beat.* MARK *moves downstage.* DAN *enters, helping* MARK *on with his coat and scarf.*]

My brother, Dan, came home from University for a few days. He's a good bloke, my brother. Bit strange, generally very OTT, but fundamentally a very kind person.

DAN   Thanks.

MARK   The day after Boxing Day I took Dan on a tour of St Anne's shopping centre, which had just opened in Harrow. We also paid homage to the new 'Sally: Statue of a Skipping Girl', which had been erected in the town centre, presumably in order to serve as a focus for community activity.

[MARK *and* DAN *stand as if looking at the statue.*]

Ah, at last Harrow's position on the cultural map is assured.

DAN   Indeed, indeed.

MARK   I'm finding it hard to hold in my tears of joy, Dan.

DAN   Let them out, Mark, let them out. It's what the artist would have wanted. Is it the two small holes which have been Black-and-Deckered into the eyeballs which moved you so, dear brother?

MARK   Indeed, indeed. They communicate so clearly the artist's idea of the glee that a child can find in simple things. [*Beat.*] Dan?

DAN   Yes?

MARK   Do you know what I'd like to do more than any-
       thing in the whole world?

DAN   No, dear brother, no.

MARK   I'd like to smear a turd in Sally's face.

DAN   Next time, dear Mark, next time we will bring a
       turd in a bag.

MARK   It's what the artist would have wanted.

DAN   Quite.

MARK   Dan?

DAN   Yes?

MARK   Is something wrong? You seem somewhat distant
       these holidays.

DAN   I've . . . I've come home for a reason.

MARK   What?

       [DAN *is silent and then about to speak when
       an* OLD FRIEND *appears.*]

FRIEND Dan, is that you?

DAN   Of course it's me. How are you?

       [*He flings his arms around the* OLD FRIEND
       and kisses her on both cheeks, a ritual that
       MARK *finds odd.*]

FRIEND Fine, fine.

DAN   Listen – have you got time for a carrot cake?

       [*He and his* OLD FRIEND *exit, chatting.*]

MARK   [*to the audience*] Poor Dan – I love him dearly but
       he's got no social skills, that boy.

Scene 3

The changing room.

MARK   By the start of the Lent term it had become evi-
dent that schoolgirls were too easy for Barry.

> [MARK *and* BARRY *are together again, sitting
> on their favourite bench.*]

What you need is a more serious challenge. Now,
as you seem to find an ejaculation during the lunch
hour an essential prerequisite for mental health
– it'll have to be someone who works within the
school grounds.

BARRY   Sounds interesting.

MARK   We'll make a list of every possibility.

BARRY   OK.

> [MARK *takes a pen and exercise book out of
> his schoolbag and is poised ready to write
> down all the possible names.*]

MARK   Kitchen staff?

BARRY   Ugly and thick.

MARK   Cleaning ladies?

BARRY   Ugly and dirty.

MARK   Mrs Webb, the physics teacher?

BARRY   Ugly and inhuman.

MARK   Right . . . French teachers, Mrs Thomas?

BARRY   Ugly and no tits.

MARK Mrs Mumford?

BARRY Not too ugly.

> [*Finally* MARK *gets to write down a name.*]

MARK Miss Gall?

BARRY Unspeakably ugly.

MARK Headmaster's wife?

BARRY Ugly and old.

MARK Librarian?

BARRY Ugly and boring.

MARK Assistant librarian?

BARRY Ugly and . . . male!

MARK Shit, sorry . . . well . . . that's it.

> [*They both look at the one name* MARK *has written down.*]

BARRY What's she like?

MARK Bland overworked housewife.

BARRY Killer tits, though.

MARK She put someone in detention once for staring at them.

BARRY What?

MARK A couple of years ago, boy in my French class, couldn't take his eyes off them.

BARRY [*amused*] What was the offence on the detention card?

MARK 'Excessive attention to irrelevant detail.'

BARRY You're kidding.

MARK Nope.

BARRY But that's hilarious – she's got a sense of humour.

MARK   Indeed, and ever since then she's been accorded some respect, partly for the beauty of her breasts but mainly for that one witticism which showed the faintest glimmer of humanity. That one joke which was only ever read by two people – the tit-starer and the detention-master – changed the way everyone thinks about her. Boys often get dangerously horny in her classes – not all the gooey lumps under the desks are chewing gum.

BARRY   But how to . . .

MARK   Seduce her? How indeed! The art of seduction, my friend, is an extremely delicate one. Unless, that is, you're you, in which case it's a piece of piss.

BARRY   [*unconvinced*] Sure.

MARK   Here's the plan. We find out where Mrs Mumford parks, then, every day for a week, after the final bell, you lean sexily against a nearby wall, ogling her as she gets into her car to drive home. Then, for two days, you don't turn up. On the following day, just as she's beginning to wonder where you've got to, you hobble up to her, tell her you've injured your foot, and ask for a lift to Stanmore, which is where she lives. Then, on a secluded spot of the A41, you suddenly shout, 'Stop! Stop the car! I'm car-sick.' She stops the car at the next lay-by. You breathe deeply as if in pain. Then, without a word, get out of the passenger seat.

BARRY   Still limping.

MARK   Forget the fucking limp. Move into the back of the car. 'Please,' you say, 'please, my head is in agony. Oh, the pain! Will you massage my temples?' She will then get into the back seat and begin massaging your temples. A few minutes later you say you feel a bit better and offer to massage her temples. You then ask her if her breasts are at all sore and offer to massage them too. The next step is that as soon as you can tell she's getting excited, let go of her tits and shout, 'Oh, shit! My lower abdomen is playing up again. Will you massage it for me?' After that you ought to be home and wet.

BARRY How long have you had this plan?

MARK Well, it was originally supposed to be for me. But you can have it.

BARRY Thanks.

MARK Barry?

BARRY Yes?

MARK What's sex like?

BARRY Um . . . God . . . er . . . it's nice.

MARK How nice?

BARRY Um . . . very nice.

MARK Shit. I thought so . . . Is it easy?

BARRY What, easy to learn or easy to do once you know how?

MARK Fuck! Good point. Fuck! I'd never thought of that. Er . . . both, I suppose.

BARRY Well – it all depends, really. First time's a bit tricky, but after that it's really no hassle at all. And once you know how . . . well, as long as you find the other person attractive, you can't go wrong, really.

MARK   Right, I see. That's amazing. I see. And is there any practice you can do to make the first time a bit easier?

BARRY   Like what?

MARK   Well – I've heard that a milk bottle filled with chopped liver is exactly the same as a vagina. Is that true?

BARRY   I don't know, I've never put my dick in a milk bottle filled with chopped liver.

MARK   Oh, I have. It's very nice.

BARRY   What! You've fucked a milk bottle filled with chopped liver?

MARK   Yes. Well, sort of.

BARRY   What do you mean, sort of?

MARK   Well – I couldn't come. That's why I'm a bit worried. It made me think that maybe I wouldn't be able to come in a woman either.

BARRY   I see. I wouldn't worry too much. Women are much nicer than milk bottles, I assure you.

MARK   Fuck! Yes, you're right. I'm so stupid. You're right. I shouldn't worry too much. Jesus, I'm such a worrier.

BARRY   Maybe if you're worried that you don't find women attractive you should think about having sex with a man.

MARK   What! Fuck off! . . . Fucking hell! . . . Fuck! . . . What are you talking about? I didn't say that! That's not what I said at all, you fucking weirdo.

BARRY   All right, all right. Calm down. It's nothing to get so excited about. I just mentioned it, that's all.

MARK   Well don't.

BARRY   Jesus – there's no need to be so homophobic.

MARK   I'm not homophobic. I'm just not a fucking arse-bandit, that's all.

BARRY   You are so screwed up. You've got such a problem.

MARK   I have not got a problem. You're the one who brought up the subject. You're the one we should be worried about.

BARRY   Worried?

MARK   Yeah – worried, Barry. You mentioned it – where did you get the idea from anyway?

BARRY   From my uncle. He's gay.

MARK   Fuck! You know one?

BARRY   Yes I do and he's a very nice man.

MARK   Ugh, yuck – it's in your genes.

BARRY   Oh Mark, please don't be such an arsehole.

MARK   No, don't you be such an arsehole.

BARRY   You're the arsehole.

MARK   No – you're the arsehole.

BARRY   You're the fucking arsehole.

MARK   [*to the audience*] It wasn't usually like that. I think you must have caught us on a bad day.

    [*Music – loud disco.* MARK, *slightly the worse for drink, wobbles in the coloured light of a sixth form disco. He shouts out at other party-goers who, we imagine, pass him by and ignore him. A lonely* GIRL *dances around her handbag.*]

Have you seen Barry? . . . Barry? Barry? You know,
body of a god, face of an angel . . . name of a
plasterer . . . ? Bastard hasn't turned up.

[*The music segues into something slow.*]

Why isn't anyone lunging at me and trying to suck
my teeth out? Why is no one slobbering noisily
over my unwashed cock?

[*He drinks down a full glass of colourful liquid
in one gulp before noticing that the* GIRL *is
watching him. Eventually he crosses over to
her and lunges at her. They break apart almost
immediately, having clashed teeth.*]

Shit!

[*He lunges at the* GIRL *again. They begin a long
snog. He breaks away again to wipe the saliva
from his chin and then re-engages. Clearly
getting bored, he manoeuvres the* GIRL *onto a
seat and begins to tear away at her clothes.
She offers some resistance but* MARK *meets
this with greater force until the two are
engaged in what looks like a full-scale arm
wrestle. The unfortunate* GIRL'*s arm eventually gives way, sending* MARK'*s fist straight
into her groin.*]

Fuck!

[*The* GIRL *is motionless and open-mouthed in
shock.* MARK *looks at her in amazement as
she eventually gets up and, bent double, exits.
The music suddenly stops and the lights snap
up.* BARRY'*s laugh can be heard as the scene
changes back to the changing room.*]

BARRY   You did what?

MARK   Punched her in the vagina. Not just a baby punch, either – this was a full-scale upper cut impeccably placed and timed, planting itself firmly right slap bang on her vag.

BARRY   What did she do?

MARK   She didn't scream with pain, just looked shocked.

BARRY   What did you do?

MARK   Marvelled at the resilience of vaginas. They must be a lot tougher than testicles. That's a blessing at least.

[BARRY *laughs.*]

Why don't you go to parties?

BARRY   Probably because they're shit.

MARK   Right.

BARRY   Why? Do you like them?

MARK   No. I think they're shit.

BARRY   Why do you go then?

MARK   Dunno.

BARRY   You must have a reason.

MARK   No. I just go.

BARRY   Oh.

MARK   I hate them though. I really hate them.

BARRY   Because they're shit?

MARK   Yeah. Because they're shit. Because they're really shit. Fuck, they really are shit. They are so shit. Fuck! So shit! Fuck! Now I think about it . . . Fuck! They're so shit. So bad. Just so, so shit! Fuck!

BARRY   You're very articulate when you have a spiritual revelation. Has anyone ever told you that before?

MARK   They're so shit.

BARRY   Why do you go then, you twat?

MARK   I don't know. Why the fuck do I go?

BARRY   Snogs?

MARK   Yes. In theory, yes. But I don't get many and I don't even enjoy them when I do.

BARRY   Shit. Maybe I should put you in touch with my uncle.

MARK   Very funny. Maybe you should.

BARRY   Look, Mark, of course you don't enjoy licking the tonsils of some pissed stranger you don't like. It's repulsive.

MARK   Is it?

BARRY   Of course it fucking is.

MARK   So I'm not meant to enjoy it.

BARRY   Well – you are meant to enjoy it. That does tend to be the idea behind these things. But if you don't enjoy it, you shouldn't do it.

MARK   Don't be an arsehole. I can't just give up on women two weeks short of my eighteenth birthday. It's a bit early for that.

BARRY   I'm not saying you should give up on women. I'm saying you should give up on adolescent groping.

MARK   What else is there for me to do? I am adolescent, and I only know how to grope.

BARRY   All I'm saying is groping or foreplay on its own with someone you love is nice – foreplay followed by sex with someone you love is great – foreplay followed by sex with someone you don't love is OK – foreplay without sex with someone you don't even like when you're pissed in a room full of other people, with neither party willing to remove any clothing, is a fucking disastrously unpleasurable experience.

MARK Fuck! I can't believe this! You were a virgin two months ago!

BARRY I'm a quick learner.

MARK Jesus. You're so right! I can't believe it. I'm such an idiot. Shit! What do I do now? What the fuck do I do now?

BARRY Dunno. Whatever you want.

MARK Shit!

BARRY Listen – this weekend, why don't we go to the cinema together, or something?

MARK Really? Do you really want to? I mean . . . shall we? I mean, yes. Yes. Let's.

BARRY All right. Calm down.

MARK Right. Yes. What do you want to see?

BARRY *The Fly II* has just come out.

MARK Naah. Horror's not really my scene. Bit boring. How about *Four Adventures of Reinette and Mirabelle* at the Everyman?

BARRY God – you *are* gay.

Scene 4

A corridor at school.

MARK The first hiccup of summer term came when I drank a glass of water too quickly. The second came when Barry told me my nickname was Bruno in honour of my now legendary vaginal thump and that he and Mrs Mumford, the French teacher, were lovers.

BARRY We've been having a passionate affair. She wants to leave her husband and family and get a flat with me in Notting Hill.

MARK But . . . but . . . you can't.

BARRY Why?

MARK Because . . . because . . . what about me?

BARRY What about you?

MARK I mean us. What about us?

BARRY What?

MARK I mean our friendship. I thought we were friends.

BARRY And?

MARK Um . . .

BARRY We are friends. So what?

MARK Um . . . you just can't. What about me? It's not fair.

BARRY It's got nothing to do with you. I'll still see you, Mark. You won't even notice the difference. I've been with her for the last six months and you didn't notice anything. Why is it going to make any difference to our friendship now?

MARK   The cinema . . .

BARRY What?

MARK   The cinema. You won't be able to go with me to the cinema any more.

BARRY Of course I will, you prat. As long as no one else in the school finds out we're living together, it won't make any difference to anyone except me and her.

MARK   But . . . shit! . . . It's not fair.

BARRY What the fuck are you twittering on about?

MARK   Wittering. The word's 'wittering', you cunt. [*Beat.*] What about her family? You're destroying her family.

BARRY I know. I think she should stay with them, but she is adamant that she wants to leave. Apparently her husband's a lazy shithead and it's about time he did some of the work with the children.

MARK   But – but – what a bitch! She can't do that, she should stay with her family.

BARRY Yes – I agree, for the kids' sake.

MARK   But . . . you can't persuade her to stay then?

BARRY I've tried but she says she can't get enough of my body and she has to have me all of the time. [*Beat.*] One day I think we'll have a child together.

[MARK *opens his mouth to speak but nothing comes out.*]

I hope it's a girl.

[MARK *faints.*]

[*Music.*]

Scene 5

Lights up on the classroom. MARGARET *(Mrs Mumford) is writing on the blackboard. She stops and stares at it for what seems like an eternity. The class (made up of* BARRY, MARK *and two others) sense something exciting in the air.* MARGARET *eventually turns to face the class, apparently calm.*

MARGARET   I am aware of certain rumours circulating in the sixth form about a sexual relationship between myself and Barry. These rumours are not only potentially damaging to myself, my career and my family, they are also . . . [*Pause.*] . . . true. I am, I must admit, having an affair – an extremely passionate affair – with one of my students. I realise that this could result in my getting the sack, and I have tried to terminate our relationship, but – well – when I see him . . . [*Long pause.*] . . . and his beautiful face, I just can't turn him away.

> [*Completely still, she closes her eyes for what seems like a minute or more. When she finally opens them again, her eyes are moist and shiny.*]

When he touches me, I can't resist him. It feels so good – it makes me feel young.

> [*She smiles to herself, obviously miles away.*]

I feel alive. He's so gentle, so tender. My husband was always a brute – his clumsy fat fingers used to maul me – I never felt a spark. But when Barry touches me, my whole body feels on fire. I feel like I'm lost – I forget everything – we move together like . . . like . . .

[*She savours the moment before her eyes snap wide open.*] (Dreams)

Listen – listen – I deserve a bit of happiness. I am fed up with . . . with all the shit. I have had enough of working twice as hard as all the other teachers in this place, who are all, of course, lazy men. I have had enough of clearing up all the shitty mess my stupid husband leaves around our boring house. I am fed up with boring children complaining about boring, stupid problems – so fuck it. Fuck it all. I, for once, am staking a claim for something I deserve. I've earned it, for God's sake, and I'm not going to take any more shit from anyone. Yes – I'm still going to mark your essays, but I'm not going to cover them in comments you can't even be bothered to read – yes – I'm still going to look after my kids, but I'm not going to cook every fucking mouthful that ever crosses their fat, spoiled lips – and no – my husband can just go screw. So I have moved out and I am living with Barry, who I love, and who is kind to me.

[*She closes her eyes again, breathes deeply and takes stock.*]

I'm sorry – I didn't mean to go into all of that. I hope I haven't embarrassed you all – but I think you understand what I mean. What I wanted to say was just this – I am having an affair with Barry, and if these rumours spread to the staff, I'll get the sack, so I'm asking you a favour. I want you, my favourite class, to kill the rumours for me. Only a few people know at the moment, and I'm sure that between you, you know who they are. I want you to explain to them my situation – I want you to tell them what I have told you. This is the only time I have ever been so honest in my whole life. I would never have thought it possible that I could be so happy. Please, explain to people my situation – I need this job if I want to live without my husband. I hope you understand. I know I shouldn't trust you, but you are Barry's friends, so I'm taking a gamble. If you're anything like Barry, I know I'm safe. Thank you – thank you for helping me. I'll go now so you have some time to think about it.

[*She leaves.*]

MARK   [*to the audience*] Two hours later, one thousand, three hundred boys knew every detail of Mrs Mumford's sex life. Within a week, she got the sack. Barry was expelled. No one knew exactly how they got together because Barry never let on – but the car seduction story I happened to let slip might as well have been true – the whole school believed it.

[*Music.*]

Scene 6

Lights up on MARGARET's *flat. She has changed from her severe work clothes to a flowing caftan – in an attempt to look younger.*

MARK   Oh my God. Have you just got out of the shower? I can come back later.

MARGARET   No! It's a caftan. I've left all my clothes at my husband's house, I didn't want to bring anything with me. I was going to have a symbolic burning of the clothes I was wearing on my final day, but I couldn't find anywhere safe so I threw them in a skip on Portobello Road. I'm compiling a new wardrobe from the shops of Notting Hill.

MARK   Your optimism is admirable.

BARRY   Doesn't she look beautiful now?

MARK   Yes, she looks . . . um . . . admirable.

MARGARET   [*pleading for more flattery*] Thank you.

> [*She goes to sit with* BARRY. *They snuggle up close to each other.*]

MARK   Yes, you look . . . um . . . you look . . . [*finally forcing himself*] . . . twenty years younger.

MARGARET   Do you really think so?

BARRY   Of course you do, everyone keeps telling you so.

MARK   Are you going to look for another teaching job?

MARGARET   [*trying too hard*] Fuck teaching!

MARK   Are you going to look for another school?

BARRY   Fuck school.

MARGARET   Barry and I are going to spend the summer fruit-picking in all the most interesting parts of the country, then I'm going to blow my savings on a trip for the two of us to India. October's the best time to go – just after the monsoon. We can stay through the winter – living in grotty hotels, eating cheap food –

MARK   Then what?

MARGARET   What do you mean, then what?

MARK   Then what – what will you do?

MARGARET   Oh, for God's sake, don't be so square. 'Then what' has made my life a misery.

MARK   I see. [*deliberately getting it wrong*] But what will you do when you get back from China?

MARGARET   India, not China.

MARK   But how will you make a living? What about Barry's education?

MARGARET   Jesus! Don't be so middle-aged.

> [*Pause while* MARK *takes a deep breath and plans his next attack.*]

MARK   How old were you in the sixties?

MARGARET   Why do you ask?

MARK   You must have been in your teens, right?

MARGARET   Yes.

MARK   And I suppose you had a really wild time.

MARGARET   Well . . . sort of.

MARK   Were you really into the Beatles?

MARGARET Yes – everyone was.

MARK It must have been amazing to see them live.

MARGARET Live?

MARK Live. You know – in concert.

MARGARET Oh. Live. Well – I never actually made it to one of their concerts. What are you on about any–?

MARK Right. Were you too spaced out on drugs or something?

MARGARET Not exactly.

MARK Were you on the hippie trail to India, then? Or passed out in a police station in Marrakech?

MARGARET No.

MARK Or maybe you were having sex on acid in Hyde Park?

MARGARET No.

MARK Or were you by any chance revising hard for your modern languages exams at Cambridge University?

MARGARET Um . . . well . . . I suppose something a little more along those lines.

MARK What degree did you get?

MARGARET A First.

MARK From Cambridge?

MARGARET From Cambridge.

MARK In which year?

MARGARET 1965.

MARK I see. There was still half the decade left, though. What about '67 – the summer of love and all that?

MARGARET Summer '67. Um ... that was ... doing up a starter home in Finchley.

MARK With your husband?

MARGARET With my husband.

MARK Who was also from Cambridge?

MARGARET Who was also from Cambridge.

MARK What degree did he get?

MARGARET A First.

MARK In what?

MARGARET Economics.

MARK Then what?

MARGARET A job.

MARK In the City?

MARGARET In the City.

MARK While you looked after the –

MARGARET Yes.

[*An embarrassed silence.*]

BARRY I think it's good to catch up on what you've missed.

[*Another embarrassed silence.*]

MARK Besides, you can't go fruit-picking this summer, Barry, because of our pact.

BARRY What pact?

MARK The day. You know – at that place.

BARRY What place?

MARK The place. You know – London.

BARRY Where in London?

MARK The middle. You know – the West End.

BARRY   What?

MARK   You remember. We were walking round Leicester Square that day after the film, and we made a pact that this July we would spend a month inter-railing together in Europe, then we went to the pub and you drank a lot and passed out.

BARRY   Are you sure?

MARK   Of course I'm fucking sure, can't you remember? I've already bought my ticket.

BARRY   Oh no.

MARK   I can't believe you'd forget a thing like that. Jesus, Barry, you can be so selfish sometimes.

BARRY   I'm sorry, Mark, I just forgot. I must have drunk too much.

MARK   So, because you get drunk once, I have to spend the whole summer trudging round Europe on my own. You bastard, Barry.

BARRY   Oh no, I'm really sorry. Mags – what am I going to do?

[MARGARET *looks up. Her eyes are wet.*]

MARGARET   Go. I'll buy you a ticket. Mark's right – I need a little time to sort myself out. A month on my own will do me good. I'll need to sort out a lawyer to deal with my husband. I have to work something out with my kids. And I still haven't told my parents what I've done. Oh God, my life's a mess. I'm out of control. I'm an idiot.

[*She begins to cry, inconsolably.*]

[*Music.*]

[MARK *does a very bad job of hiding his delight.
Eventually he motions to* BARRY, *miming a
drinking gesture as an invitation to go down
the pub.* BARRY *leaves* MARGARET, *still cry-
ing. He and* MARK *take one look at her before
dashing out.*]

[*Lights fade on* MARGARET.]

Scene 7

Lights bounce up on MARK.

MARK   The next day I went straight to my local temping
agency to sign up for a job. I turned up at the
offices of Lentrust Insurance Services at nine
o'clock the next morning. I had been told by friends
that working as a filing clerk was boring, but this
was truly an extraordinary experience. I spent
most of my day at the end of the room where the
telephone answering girls worked.

[*Lights up on a telephone answering* GIRL,
*wearing a headset. Her switch from cockney
gossip to 'telephone voice' is seamless. As she
speaks we imagine we are sitting next to her
and the other girls.*]

GIRL   My mate Sal told me that her Tone took her up
the shitter once and it did absolutely nothing for
her hello Lentrust Insurance Services can I help
you? Jesus I said to her Jesus I wouldn't want a

bloke with a dick that size I mean it's bound to
do you some serious hello Lentrust Insurance
Services can I help you? Not when I'm on at least
not usually blocked dishwasher? You want 427–
2375 madam fucks up the sheets doesn't it? Here
did you read that thing about the woman and the
horse? Have you still got a copy of the guaran-
tee? Apparently she had to go to hospital she'll
probably have half-horse half-baby only one year
for a hairdryer I'm afraid bet the horse loved it
though.

[*Blackout.*]

[*Music.*]

Scene 8

MARGARET's *flat. Background music.* BARRY *comes
through from the kitchen, wearing an apron and stir-
ring something in a saucepan.*

BARRY   Everyone all right with goat's cheese? Because
I can use cheddar if you like but it'll lose some
piquancy.

MARGARET   Sounds delicious.

MARK   Um . . . fine.

BARRY   Good.

[*He disappears into the kitchen again.*]

[*off*] Mark, you don't have a nut allergy, do you?

MARK   [*under his breath*] I'm rapidly developing one. [*shouting to* BARRY] No. [*Pause.*] Margaret?

MARGARET   Yes?

MARK   What kind of relationship did you have with your mother?

MARGARET   Um . . . fine. Why do you ask?

MARK   Just wondering.

MARGARET   Oh.

MARK   Did she ever desert you as a child at any stage?

MARGARET   No.

> [MARK *is in psychoanalyst mode and moves behind the reclining* MARGARET.]

MARK   If you think back, are you absolutely sure?

MARGARET   Positive.

MARK   Was she a good mother? Did she breast-feed you?

MARGARET   Yes, she was an OK mother, and I don't really remember if she breast-fed me – I was a bit young at the time.

MARK   Ah – sarcasm as a defence mechanism. Interesting. So you don't feel neglected in any way?

MARGARET   No, of course not.

MARK   Are you sure?

MARGARET   Actually – now I come to think of it, there was this one time . . . yes . . . God, I must have been about twelve. My father came home drunk and started touching me in funny ways. When my mother tried to protect me, he hit her. I remember clearly now. The back of his fist smashed on her nose – I remember blood spattering out onto

my dress. She screamed, picked up a large saucepan and hit him over the head with it. He was
knocked out cold, and he toppled to the ground,
falling on top of me. I couldn't move but my mother
dragged me from under him – it hurt my leg and
I remember it tore my dress. A little tear, just above
the waist.

[MARK *is aghast.*]

She pulled me out of the house – it was raining
hard – and we just ran away – I don't know where
to – I was scared – we just ran. It was only when
we were halfway to the railway station that she
remembered my sisters, so we turned round and
went home.

MARK   Jesus Christ!

MARGARET Ever since then I've had a suppressed agony – a
fear of the adult world – of parenthood. I've always
known that I could never be a good mother.

[*She hides her face and starts to shake. There
is a long pause as* MARK *takes it all in before
he begins to notice she is shaking with laughter, not tears. She bursts into hysterics.*]

Oh Mark, you're so gullible. I never would have
taken you for such a dunce. [*wiping the corners of
her eyes*] It's sweet, you're so transparent. I love
young men.

[MARK *is furious and gets up to leave.* BARRY
*comes in from the kitchen with a bottle of wine
and some glasses.*]

MARK   I didn't believe you, I'm not stupid. Fucking bitch!

[*He storms out.*]

BARRY   What's up with him?

MARGARET   [*still smiling*] Hurt pride – he'll be all right when
           he cools down.

BARRY   Well, I hope he does it quickly. I don't fancy spend-
           ing four weeks with him in one of his mega sulks.

MARGARET   I wish you didn't have to go. I'm going to miss
           you.

BARRY   I'm going to miss you too, flopsy bunny.

MARGARET   You will call sometimes, won't you? Let me know
           you're OK?

BARRY   Every day.

           [*The music swells and he kisses her delicately
           as the lights cross-fade.*]

Scene 9

           MARK *is picked up in a spot. He is wearing sunglasses
           and an appropriate 'return from holiday' T-shirt.*

MARK   Returning from Europe, I needed to spend a month
           in solitary confinement in order to regain a taste
           for humanity. I thought frequently about how
           much I hated Barry, his habits, the things he says,
           the way he smells of almonds. I never wanted to
           see him again – it was nearly five days before I
           called in on him . . .

           [*The lights open up to reveal* MARGARET'*s flat.*

BARRY *and* MARGARET *stand looking at one another, silently. She has a suitcase. He is in a trance.*]

MARGARET Not a good time, Mark.

MARK Why? What's happening?

MARGARET Perhaps you could call back in an hour or so.

MARK Bit difficult for me, actually, because . . .

MARGARET Just go, Mark!

[*Finally getting the message,* MARK *begins to back off.*]

BARRY No!

MARGARET What?

BARRY I want him to stay.

MARGARET Barry, I have some things I need to say to you. Private things. Mark, please, just give us a moment.

MARK I don't think Barry wants me to go, do you, Barry?

[BARRY *shakes his head.*]

Sorry.

[*He sits down.*]

MARGARET Very well. [*takes a deep breath*] Barry, don't think that I don't love you. You mustn't ever think that I don't care for you with all my heart. I love you as much as my own children. But we can't carry on like this. Loving you was the best thing that happened to me, but that's all it was – a thing that happened to me.

[BARRY, *who up until now has remained impassive, flinches at this.*]

Oh God, I had this all prepared, now it's coming out wrong. Look, some people are women of passion, brave women, irresponsible women; others are women of duty, caring women with responsibilities and duties, and I'm one of those. You showed me a new side of my character – one that can laugh and scream and be spontaneous and have orgasms, but a month on my own to think about things has shown me that this is not who I am. I salute you for what you have taught me and I wish I could have been a more receptive student for your lessons of love. Now I have begged and pleaded with the school, explaining that the fault was all mine, and they have agreed to take you back as a student for the upper sixth. I will be seeking employment elsewhere. You will always be with me in my heart.

[*She leaves.*]

MARK   The bitch!

[*Long pause.* BARRY *turns and wordlessly walks away, eventually slumping down.* MARK *stops just short of giving him a hug and puts a manly hand on his shoulder instead.*]

Fucking women. They're all the same. They all shit on you in the end.

[*His words have no effect on* BARRY.]

You'll find another one. There's plenty more fi–

[*He stops himself.*]

BARRY   I can't believe that she'd . . .

MARK   Do that to you?

BARRY Do you think she was . . . a little old for me?

MARK Do I think she was a little old for you?

BARRY Yes. Do you?

MARK Well . . . I mean, it's difficult to say at this stage.
I suppose if you're sexually compatible there's
nothing to stop you having a fulfilling relationship. I mean, if you found her attractive there's
no reason not to . . . um . . . most people don't find
women that old at all sexy, but if you . . . not that
she wasn't fantastic, I mean, she was an exception for her age . . . I mean, very well preserved
and all that . . . so once you're over the attraction
hurdle you can . . . um . . . How old's your mother
exactly?

BARRY What?

MARK Just – how old's your mum?

BARRY What do you mean?

MARK Nothing. Nothing at all. I just wondered.

BARRY My mum's sort of forty-five or something like that.
But I haven't got a thingy complex, if that's what
you mean.

MARK Are you sure?

BARRY Of course I'm fucking sure. I haven't wanted to
shag my mum for years.

MARK You never know, though. That's the whole
point. It's subconscious. I thought I'd grown out
of wanting to shag my mum, but only the other
week I had a dream where she looked like Kim
Basinger and bingo – it was hard-on city.

BARRY Your mum doesn't look anything like Kim Basinger.

MARK I know. I don't know how she did it! It was incred-
      ible. But I dreamed it. So you don't need to be Freud
      to know that my subconscious wants me to have
      sex with my mother.

BARRY What did your mum do in this dream to turn you
      on so much?

MARK Oh . . . er . . . I can't . . . um . . . remember the
      details, really.

BARRY Shit! That's so embarrassing. Did your mum know
      that you were turned on?

MARK No, she couldn't see. I was hiding my dick behind
      a pocket dictionary. Look – it's not important.
      The point is, my subconscious put a nice face and
      big tits onto my mother in order to trick me into
      fancying her.

BARRY You can't have been that turned on if you could
      hide your whole dick behind a pocket dictionary.

MARK Will you shut up about my fucking dream! I wish
      I hadn't told you now.

BARRY Actually, now you come to mention it, I did have
      a weird dream a few weeks ago.

MARK What?

BARRY In it, I'm a little kid, and I'm in my bedroom, and
      my mum comes in and starts teaching me French
      verbs. Then I tell her that I need a pee, and she
      carries me to the toilet and holds me in the air to
      make me tall enough to get it into the bowl, but I
      can't produce a proper wee. All that comes out is
      these little dollops. I don't know what they are,
      and I get scared, but my mum is kind and holds
      me there and just keeps saying that it doesn't

matter and I can try again. But all that comes out is white dollops.

MARK Jesus!

BARRY I didn't think twice at the time, but now . . .

MARK You didn't think twice at the time! What are you, an idiot?

BARRY No – you know how it is. You just, you know, wake up, think you're a pervert for a few seconds, then forget the whole thing ever happened.

MARK Fuck!

BARRY You think I'm better off without her?

MARK Yeah – of course you are. You're young – you should be playing the field. Not sitting in a flat with a twisted wife/mother figure, storing up a lifetime of mother-shagging trauma for yourself. Jesus, for a while there you were well into Bates' Motel territory.

BARRY You could be right. I did love her, though.

MARK Who? Margaret or your mother?

BARRY Margaret, you tosser.

MARK Just checking.

[*Music.*]

Scene 10

MARK's *house.* BARRY *and* MARK *are interrupted by* LOUISE, BARRY's *sister.*

LOUISE   So you're Mark. You don't look that bad. Barry tells me you nick biros, pick your nose and smell of almonds.

MARK   It's him that smells of almonds.

BARRY   He's right. I smell of almonds. Mark's the one with asparagus pants.

MARK   My pants do . . .

> [LOUISE *laughs.* MARK *stops himself and looks at* BARRY *as if to say 'Who's she?'*]

BARRY   My sister, Louise.

> [*The lights close down on* MARK.]

MARK   Barry has a sister! Fuck! I immediately decided she's the one for me. I know what you're thinking. I'm sorry to spoil the fun of your sordid speculations but the time has come to break the news – I am not, and never will be, a successful homosexual. The really weird thing was that now that I had decided to make absolutely sure I was 100 percent straight, all of a sudden Barry started being physically affectionate to me. Almost as soon as the thought of Barry stopped giving me hard-ons, we started sort of falling in love. I began to notice when no one was looking we walked a little closer together than usual – side by side, but with our shoulders brushing in a way that wasn't normal. We never talked about it. I couldn't tell if it was me or him, but one of us must have been aware of it because when we got back into a public place we stopped doing it. I couldn't figure out how or why or in what way we were in love. It was odd – it was physical, but not sexual. Which is odd, because if it was physical, then it was obviously a bit sexual, but it didn't seem sex-sexual, just friendly sexual. Anyway, none of this shit really matters. Fuck me, I'm beginning to sound like Mrs Mumford!

> [*The lights bounce up again to reveal the three of them together again.*]

BARRY   Must dash – I'll be gone for at least an hour.

LOUISE   That was subtle, Barry.

> [BARRY *exits.* LOUISE *and* MARK *stand looking at one another.*]

So what shall we do?

> [MARK *giggles.*]

Do you want to go upstairs?

MARK   Well, it's been a week now, I think we've reached the stage in our relationship when making love seems the right thing to do.

LOUISE   Your bedroom. Five minutes.

> [*She leaves.*]

MARK   [*as he follows her*] Jesus, hurry, I've got a concrete erection, I'm worried about creating a whole new chapter in the history of premature ejaculation

by spunking in my trousers halfway up the stair-
case . . .

[*Blackout.*]

[*Music.*]

[*Lights up to reveal* LOUISE *and* MARK *in bed.*
MARK *is looking under the covers.*]

MARK   I've never seen it so small. Well, maybe once trying to have a pee during a snowball fight at the
age of five, but other than that, this is definitely a
record.

LOUISE   It's all right, you're bound to be afraid first time.

MARK   *How* do you know it's my first time? I mean, how
do you *know* it's my first time?

LOUISE   Barry told me.

MARK   Jesus. Thanks, Barry. [*looking under the covers
again*] God, it's shrunk even more.

LOUISE   That's one of the reasons I like you so much.

MARK   I'm sorry. I don't understand.

LOUISE   I like the way you are. You're not old and cynical. You're fun. You're transparent.

MARK   What! What the fuck do you mean, transparent?

LOUISE   All right – don't get angry. It's a compliment. Look
– all my life I've gone out with older men. When
I was . . . when I was fourteen, I lost my virginity
with a thirty-one-year-old. Since then, the men
have got a bit younger, but they have always,
always, been older than me. And I'm fed up with
boring, world-weary, cynical, rich men who pay
for everything and tell me what to do. I'm just
bored of it.

MARK Sounds all right to me.

LOUISE Look – I had a bit of a . . . well, the last guy I went out with was a real bastard, and it all got so . . . well, we got into one of those self-destructive relationships where we were just punishing each other all of the time . . .

MARK Know them well.

LOUISE Barry's been talking about you such a lot, and saying such nice things about you. He really respects you so much, you know. And everything he said made me feel a lot of warmth for you. It was as if I fell in love with you before I even met you. And when you first came round and you were all coy – it was just so sweet – I really . . . you know . . . I just like how you are.

MARK Great, I'm really flattered that you find me attractive because I'm coy and transparent. Thanks.

LOUISE No no no no, you've got completely the wrong idea. I want you because . . . because . . .

MARK I'm Barry's friend?

LOUISE No – because . . . um . . .

MARK I'm inexperienced and you can boss me around?

LOUISE No – because . . . just . . . I like you. I really do.

MARK But am I . . . ? I mean, is it . . . ? Am I – am I handsome enough?

[LOUISE *laughs and gives him a kiss.*]

LOUISE I like ugly men.

MARK Damn. Not the answer I had hoped for.

[*They kiss as the lights fade.*]

[*Music.*]

[*Blackout.*]

MARK   He shoots, he scores! Goal! Brazil – Zico! Thank you, God.

[*The lights come back up again.* DAN *has joined* MARK *on the bed.*]

Don't get me wrong, Dan, everything is great – the sex is amazing, still, after a month! We get on really well, but she's only ever physical with me when we're in bed. Outside the bedroom she treats me like an ordinary friend.

DAN   Continue.

MARK   Well, it's just that I'm getting my physical affection from a guy who's thrown me into a year's worth of paranoia about my sexuality, my sex from his sister, who never touches me with my clothes on, and meanwhile, I'm sustaining an apparently normal friendship with both of them.

DAN   You've grown up a lot, Mark.

[*Music.*]

[MARK *hits him and they playfully wrestle.* DAN *pins* MARK *down and is sitting on his chest as the lights go down. When the lights come up again* DAN *has been replaced by* BARRY, *dressed in just his underwear.*]

BARRY   Brother! I didn't know you had a brother!

MARK   What do you mean?

BARRY   What do you think I mean? Since I have known you, you have never told me that you had a brother. I can't believe it!

MARK   What's so unusual about having a brother? Most people have brothers.

BARRY No – I just can't believe you haven't told me.

MARK   Why should I have told you?

BARRY What?

MARK   Well, you know, he's at university, he hardly ever comes home.

BARRY He's still your brother.

MARK   Yes, but I've barely seen him for two years, why should I have told you about him?

[DAN *re-enters, unseen.*]

BARRY You just should. He's your brother. I'm your friend. It would have been nice to know that he exists, that's all.

MARK   OK. OK. Sorry already.

BARRY Sorry already?

MARK   Sorry already.

DAN   It's an expression.

[BARRY *turns to look at him.*]

BARRY I've never heard it.

MARK   No, you wouldn't have done.

BARRY What does it mean?

DAN   It just means sorry.

BARRY Sorry already means sorry?

DAN   Yes, it's a Jewish expression.

BARRY Oh.

DAN   Oh, already.

[*He leaves.*]

BARRY Oh, already. [*to* MARK] What's he called?

MARK Dan.

BARRY Dan. What university is he at?

MARK Cambridge.

BARRY Bring him to my mum's party.

MARK You won't like him.

> [*Blackout.*]
>
> [*Music.*]
>
> [*When the lights return* MARK *and* LOUISE *are standing either side of the bed. She is wearing a dressing gown, he is naked except for a pillow, which he clutches to his groin. They are in the middle of a row.*]

LOUISE What the fuck do you think you're doing?

MARK I – I was about to ask you the same question.

LOUISE Very funny, Mark, you little runt. I was making love, what are you doing?

MARK Um . . . running away.

LOUISE Yes, and why, Mark, are you running away?

MARK Um . . .

LOUISE Well?

MARK Because I'm scared.

LOUISE And why are you scared, you little coward?

MARK Um . . .

LOUISE Well?

MARK Um . . . because . . .

LOUISE Yes?

MARK . . . because you licked my bum.

LOUISE   You are pathetic. Do you realise that? You are a typical suburban, boring, unadventurous, childish little squirt. I don't know how you can live with yourself.

MARK   I don't know how you can lick my bum.

LOUISE   You know you enjoy it.

MARK   What? Of course I don't enjoy it – it frightens the shit out of me.

LOUISE   Of course you enjoy it. You're just too repressed to admit it. There's nothing you want more in the whole world than for my gorgeous brother to take you up the arse.

MARK   What!

LOUISE   Play your cards right and you might just strike gold, too. You're far too fucked up to actually give it a go, though.

[*She storms off.* MARK *begins to get dressed.*]

MARK   You'd think a row like that would be enough to end a relationship, but we seemed to have one of these every single week. That party Barry's mum threw was incredible, best I'd ever been to – even Louise seemed to be in a good mood. When the Easter break came, Barry told me that he wanted to have a period of intense revision during the holidays, and he suggested that we hire a place in the country and go away for a week, together with his sister. Amazingly, that very evening my brother popped down from Cambridge with the very same idea . . .

[MARK *and* DAN *are now together.*]

MARK   Shit, that's incredible! Only this afternoon Barry suggested to me that I go away with him and Louise over Easter.

DAN   What a coincidence.

MARK   Listen – I've got an amazing idea, how about the four of us go away together? It'll be a lot cheaper if there's four. What do you reckon?

DAN   Gosh. What an amazing idea.

MARK   I know you don't know them and everything but you'll like them, I promise. You've met Louise, and Barry's at school with me, he's her brother.

DAN   Let me see – Barry . . . Barry . . . um . . . I think I met him at that party. Tall, dishy, blond hair.

MARK   I suppose so. That's him.

DAN   Great, that's all settled, then. I've spoken to a letting agency, and there's a place we can have in Cumbria from the third to the tenth of April which sleeps four and will only cost £45 each. You can drive up from London in Louise's car, pick me up in Cambridge, and we can all head up there together.

MARK   Fuck! You're very well organised. Brilliant . . . that's um . . . perfect . . . I suppose. I'll just check with Barry and Louise that they're happy for you to come along.

DAN   I'm sure they won't mind. We're all set, then.

MARK   Brilliant.

DAN   Excellent. I'm really looking forward to meeting Brian and Lisa again.

MARK   Barry and Louise.

DAN   That's it. I hope we all get on.

MARK Me too. You never know, really, do you?

DAN   No.

[DAN *is working hard to stop himself laughing.*]

MARK Dan? Are you all right?

DAN   Fine. Fine. Absolutely fine.

MARK You don't look it.

DAN   I'm fine . . . I . . . just . . . er . . . I'm just . . . er . . . pleased that you've come up with such a good idea.

MARK Oh, it wasn't me, really. You've done all the work. It's just a nice coincidence, really.

DAN   Yes. What a nice coincidence.

MARK Are you sure you're all right?

DAN   Hay fever, need to sneeze. I have to go.

[*He dashes off.*]

MARK Poor Dan, he's not usually like that. He must be under terrible stress.

Scene 11

The holiday cottage. There is a loud burst of laughter
from LOUISE, DAN *and* BARRY, *who are sitting around,*
after-dinner style. MARK *is looking very uncomfort-*
able and he joins in the laughter a beat too late.

DAN   Mark, do you notice anything strange here?

MARK   Yes I do, actually.

         [*Pause.*]

DAN   There's something we want to tell you.

MARK   What do you mean, we?

         [DAN *puts his head in his hands.*]

DAN   Shit, I wanted to do this nicely. I think I've given
it away already.

MARK   Given what away? Will someone tell me what
you're talking about?

DAN   Look – this holiday wasn't just a coincidence. We
planned it as a way of getting you on your own
so that we could break some important news to
you.

MARK   What? What news? And what's all this 'we' stuff?

         [*Silence.*]

LOUISE   For fuck's sake, Mark. Can't you guess? Jesus
Christ – do you have to make them say it? Just
think, for once in your life. Look at the pair of them.
Do they look like they hardly know each other?

MARK   No – they don't! What's been going on?

DAN   Mark, we got you to come here because we
       thought it might be the easiest way to tell you that
       Barry and I are . . . well, we're in love.

MARK   Oh my God! *You* two.

BARRY I'm sorry. I should have told you earlier.

MARK   Earlier? Fucking hell – how long has it been? . . .

       [*The three of them look at* MARK.]

       Dan – you're not . . . and Barry . . . Fuck. Both of
       you. I don't believe it.

       [*He looks across at* LOUISE.]

LOUISE You're a fucking moron. How can you not have
       noticed?

MARK   Noticed what? I mean, I've noticed now, but how
       could I notice? . . . I mean, what was . . . ? How
       have . . . ? Are you . . . ? Have you been . . . ? Are
       you . . . ?

DAN   Benders?

MARK   Are you?

       [DAN *and* BARRY *look at one another and reach
       out and hold hands.* MARK *wants to be sick.*]

       So have you two . . . have you two been . . . ?

BARRY Afraid so, ever since Christmas.

MARK   What! At that party? Fuck! I don't believe it. Jesus!
       Jesus Christ! Dan – you're my brother! How come
       I didn't even know! I mean, how long have you
       been . . . ? You know . . .

DAN   You can say it, it won't hurt.

MARK   Gay. How long have you been gay?

DAN   Ever since I was born, darling.

MARK   But when did you . . . ?

DAN   I came out just over a year ago in Cambridge. Barry's my first proper lover, though.

MARK   Jesus! I can't believe it! And Barry . . . you're . . . Barry . . . what the . . . ? I mean, what are you? What's going on? Are you a . . . ? Are you a . . . ?

BARRY   A what?

MARK   A bisexual – are you a bisexual?

BARRY   I don't know. I think this is what I'm really into.

[*He touches* DAN.]

At school there's a lot of pressure to conform – I think that's why I was a bit over-enthusiastic. I'm not really into the woman thing at all.

DAN   It's just a phase he went through.

MARK   Ha fucking ha. Very witty. I wish you weren't so fucking smug about the whole thing. You're both beginning to piss me off.

[DAN, *with his arm around* BARRY's *shoulder, looks at* MARK *sharply.* MARK's *confusion evaporates in an instant, turning to anger.*]

It's disgusting. Both of you – you're disgusting.

[*Silence.*]

DAN   I think you should take that back, it's very insulting.

MARK   What do you mean, take it back? You know I'm telling the truth.

DAN   [*beginning to get angry*] What?

MARK   It's disgusting. It's unnatural. You've nicked my
        best friend, and turned him into a fucking bender,
        and now you're just sitting there laughing smugly
        about how clever and different you are.

        [BARRY *stands up. He speaks calmly but is
        obviously angry too.*]

BARRY   You're jealous.

MARK   No – I'm just repulsed. You're repulsive.

BARRY   Please, Mark, don't behave like this.

MARK   It's disgusting.

        [BARRY, DAN *and* LOUISE *all look at him.*]

BARRY   You're pathetic.

MARK   *I'm* pathetic. That's a joke.

BARRY   I know why you're behaving like this.

        [MARK *grunts.*]

        Do you remember the first time we met?

MARK   No.

BARRY   It was in the changing room, after rugby, during
        my first week at school. We didn't say anything
        but that was when we became friends.

MARK   What the fuck are you talking about?

BARRY   I was getting changed and you were watching me
        with your eyes on stalks, your tongue hanging out,
        and your groin humping a schoolbag.

        [MARK *is lost for words.*]

        Do you remember?

MARK   Fuck off.

BARRY   You know I'm not making it up. Why do you think I picked you as a friend? I knew from the start that we were . . . similar.

MARK   What are you talking about? I picked you as a friend. Anyway – what do you mean, similar? Are you saying I'm gay?

BARRY   No – I'm just saying that we shared a degree of confusion. That's why we were attracted to each other.

MARK   Attracted?

BARRY   Yes!

MARK   You were attracted to me?

BARRY   Not as much as you were to me – but I thought you were OK. Have to admit – I prefer your brother.

MARK   I can't fucking believe this, everything's happening at once. It's too much.

DAN   Mark, nothing's happening at once. It's all been unfolding with exceptional slowness over the last two years, but you've just been too thick to notice anything until it's jammed down your throat. What the hell did you think I was doing spending all that time in Harrow – admiring the architecture?

MARK   I can't believe it. This is all too much. I can't believe that my brother and my best friend are both gay. It's unbelievable!

BARRY   It's not that surprising, really, you're the classic fag hag.

MARK I am not. I am not a fag hag.

       [*A pause as they all look at him.*]

       What's a fag hag?

DAN A fag hag, strictly speaking, is a woman. But it's basically any straight person who spends their time hanging around with gays in order to escape problems with their own sexuality.

MARK Fuck off! Will you all fuck off! You're the ones who are bent, so how the fuck has this turned into a character assassination of me? There's nothing wrong with me.

BARRY There's nothing wrong with us, either.

MARK Of course there is – you're shagging my fucking brother.

       [BARRY *grabs him by the shoulders, shouting into his face.*]

BARRY Oh, grow up! Will you just fucking grow up!

       [*He pushes* MARK *away and storms out.*]

       [LOUISE *storms out after* BARRY.]

       [*Music.*]

       [MARK *sits and sobs.* DAN *tries to give him a hug but* MARK *shrugs him off.*]

Scene 12

Back home in Harrow. MARK *and* DAN *face each other.*

DAN   I think we just told you in the wrong way. I didn't realise how jealous you'd be.

> [MARK *almost argues back but lets it go.*]

MARK   I really am sorry.

DAN   It's not me you have to apologise to – I can take it. Barry's very upset, though.

MARK   Why?

DAN   Well – other than Louise, you're the first person he's ever told.

MARK   And you.

DAN   He didn't have to tell me.

MARK   How did you know, then?

DAN   How do you think?

MARK   I don't know, do I. That's why I'm asking.

DAN   I just knew. It was obvious.

MARK   What, straight away?

DAN   Yes.

MARK   Are you telling me that you walked into my room, looked at Barry, my best friend for over a year, and knew straight away that he was gay?

DAN   Exactly.

MARK   Bollocks.

DAN   I reckon it took about a minute to be completely sure.

MARK   That's amazing. Have you people got a secret code or something?

DAN   We people? Have 'we people' got a secret code? If you want to call it that, yes. It's called intuition – a concept utterly alien to heterosexual men.

MARK   That's rubbish – I've got intuition. I just choose to use it on women.

DAN   Don't make me laugh. Straight men have such a hard time trying to understand themselves, they don't even think about attempting anyone else.

MARK   You're wrong, actually, I've got plenty of intuition.

DAN   Yeah, right. You and Louise – the mind-reading couple.

MARK   Maybe we are. What do you know about it?

DAN   More than you'd think.

MARK   What – more intuition?

DAN   No – gossip. Even more reliable.

MARK   What's she told you? What have you heard?

DAN   Look – you're meant to be apologising, not getting me to reveal which dismal secrets of your doomed relationship I know about. You started off wanting to know if Barry was upset.

MARK   Oh, yeah.

DAN   Aren't you going to ask?

MARK   I'm asking, for God's sake. Don't be so anal. Oh, sorry.

DAN   He's upset.

MARK   Shit. Is he angry?

DAN   Yes, very.

MARK   Really?

DAN   Of course really. It's no joke. You managed to squeeze all the worst things you could possibly have said into the two minutes before he walked out.

MARK   Really?

DAN   Will you stop saying that? I'm not lying.

MARK   Sorry.

DAN   You insulted him very badly.

MARK   Yes.

DAN   And you have to apologise.

MARK   Yes, you're right.

> [*He turns round and is now facing* LOUISE, *as if at her front door.*]

Can Barry come out? . . . I mean . . . Is Barry there?

LOUISE He doesn't want to see you. You behaved unforgivably. You're evil . . . and chucked.

> [MARK *turns back to* DAN.]

MARK   This is awful.

DAN   Yes, I'm so sorry your relationship with Louise got dragged into this.

MARK   Not her – Barry – he won't see me.

DAN   You'll just have to give him some time – then get on your hands and knees . . . and beg.

> [*Music.*]

Scene 13

The changing room. BARRY, *back in school uniform, sits on a bench. He is obviously waiting for someone.* MARK, *also in his school uniform, watches him for a moment and eventually speaks to him.*

MARK How long are we going to go on like this?

[BARRY *jumps – he was not expecting* MARK. *He gets up and looks for an exit but* MARK *has him cornered. He sits back down again.*]

It's been weeks. I've tried to apologise but you won't let me talk to you. You won't let me near you. Barry?

[*No response.*]

Barry?

[*Silence.*]

Bazza?

[*Silence.*]

Bottom?

[*A flicker of a smile.* MARK *approaches* BARRY *and touches his shoulder.*]

I'm sorry.

[BARRY *looks up and catches* MARK's *eye.*]

Barry – please. What do you want me to do, for fuck's sake?

[MARK's *eyes begin to water. This amazes* BARRY.]

BARRY   Jesus, are those tears?

[*He stands up, moves towards* MARK *and embraces him. They hold their hug until* MARK *opens his eyes and is distracted.*]

MARK   Fuck – there's someone spying on us – by that tree.

[BARRY *looks around.*]

BARRY   Oh, it's Robert.

MARK   Robert?

BARRY   Robert Levin, I'm meeting him here.

MARK   [*shouting*] Fuck off, Levin. This has got fuck all to do with you, you little cunt!

[BARRY *untangles himself from* MARK *and sits down again. He runs his fingers through his hair and lets out a snort of a laugh.*]

What?

BARRY   Dunno. At least you're consistent, I suppose.

MARK   Well, the little shit attacked me the other day. Said I was a selfish, self-obsessed, mean-spirited, homo-phobic egomaniac. What have you been saying about me, Barry?

[BARRY *doesn't respond.*]

You're meant to be my friend, you arsehole.

[*Silence.*]

Are you cheating on my brother with Levin?

[BARRY *snorts again.*]

BARRY   Nice one, Mark.

MARK   Barry, I really can't talk to you with that tosser waiting over there.

BARRY   That's OK, then, because I don't think there's a lot more to say.

MARK   What? Is that it, then? Now that you've slagged me off, you feel satisfied, do you?

BARRY   I haven't slagged you off, Mark.

MARK   I suppose that little prick made up all that stuff, then, did he?

BARRY   No.

MARK   Then you've slagged me off, haven't you? I get cross with you – once – by accident, and you just use it as an excuse to run away like a little fucking girl, choose a new prick of a best friend to hold hands with in the playground, and you giggle away together, bitching about me behind my back. You're . . . you're just . . .

BARRY   I haven't been bitching about you, Mark.

MARK   No, of course you haven't – in fact it sounds like you've been really fucking complimentary.

BARRY   I don't enjoy criticising you, Mark, I really don't. But I'm allowed to tell my friend how I feel. You never took me seriously. You always let me down. You . . .

MARK   Jesus, Barry – you're so full of hippie shit these days.

BARRY   If that's what you want to call it.

       [*Long embarrassed silence.*]

MARK   Wanker.

BARRY Tosser.

MARK Arsehole.

BARRY Prick.

MARK Poof.

BARRY Shitface.

MARK Baboon.

BARRY Platypus.

MARK Filet O'Fish.

BARRY Cuddly toy.

MARK Washing machine.

BARRY Electric ice-cube dispenser.

MARK Twig.

BARRY Abraham Lincoln's last fart in a bottle.

MARK The complete prose of Cilla Black in four volumes.

> [BARRY *smiles*.]

BARRY You do realise that I think you're an arsehole?

MARK Oh yes, I think you've made that abundantly clear.

BARRY Good.

MARK And I hope you appreciate that you're the biggest jerk I have ever met.

BARRY Absolutely.

MARK Good.

BARRY Well, I'd better . . . um . . .

MARK Of course.

> [*They stand for a moment looking at one another, smiling and not smiling at the same time, before* BARRY *leaves.*]

The strange thing is, Barry never really spoke to me again. I maintain he was just as crap towards me as I was towards him. I stand by my belief that he behaved like a little girl. I'm better off without him. I still think I could have cured him. And I do still get on with my brother, which proves that I'm not homophobic. Doesn't it?

[*Music.*]

THE END

Other playtexts published by Amber Lane Press include

CARLO ARDITO
Brief Candle/Stoney Bowes/Confessions of Zeno/Da Ponte's Last Stand
St James's Blues/A Bed for the Knight/Waiting for the Barbarians

CHARLES DYER
Lovers Dancing

RONALD HARWOOD
After the Lions
The Dresser
Interpreters
The Ordeal of Gilbert Pinfold (adapted from Evelyn Waugh)

JULIAN MITCHELL
August (a version of Chekhov's Uncle Vanya)
Falling Over England

ALAN PLATER
I Thought I Heard a Rustling

JAMES SAUNDERS
Bodies
Savoury Meringue/Who Was Hilary Maconochie?/Play for Yesterday/
Birdsong/Poor Old Simon

BRIAN THOMPSON
Turning Over

HUGH WHITEMORE
The Best of Friends
Disposing of the Body
It's Ralph
A Letter of Resignation
Stevie

For a free copy of our complete list of plays and theatre books write to:
Amber Lane Press, Church Street, Charlbury, Oxon OX7 3PR
Telephone and fax: 01608 810024   e-mail: jamberlane@aol.com